Amazing Animals of the
RAIN FOREST

Silver Dolphin Books

An imprint of the Baker & Taylor Publishing Group

10350 Barnes Canyon Road, San Diego, CA 92121

www.silverdolphinbooks.com

ISBN-13: 978-1-60710-721-7

ISBN-10: 1-60710-721-X

Manufactured, printed, and assembled in China.

3 4 5 16 15 14

LPP/04/14

Amazing Animals of the
RAIN FOREST

written by Christina Wilsdon

Silver Dolphin
San Diego, California

Contents

What Is a Rain Forest?

EQUATOR

Where can you find bats that eat fruit, lizards that fly, and parrots that hang upside down? These animals all live in rain forests. Rain forests are wet green forests that grow in a part of the world called the **tropics**.*

The tropics lie on both sides of the **equator**. The equator is an imaginary line. It goes around the earth's middle, halfway between the North and South Poles.

A tropical rain forest is warm all year long. A "chilly" day is in the high 60s—about room temperature. A hot day is in the mid-90s—like a hot summer day in parts of North America. What about the "rain" in "rain forest"? A rain forest gets about 100 inches of rain or more in one year.

*The definitions of words in **bold** can be found in the glossary on page 36.

▼Blue-and-yellow macaw

Many Different Trees

Rain forests have a wider variety of animals and plants living in them than similar habitats in other places. A patch of rain forest 4 miles long and 4 miles wide may contain 750 kinds of trees. A same-size forest in the United States may have about 10 or 15 kinds of trees.

6

That's more than twice as much rain as New York City gets. Some rain forests are soaked by up to 400 inches of rain! Warmth, sunlight, and rain create a great living place, or **habitat**, for plants. Plants grow all year round. They do not shed all their leaves in one season as plants do in many parts of Europe and North America. There are a great many animals in rain forests, too. More than half of the world's different kinds, or **species**, of plants and animals live in rain forests. People live and work in rain forests, too.

Rain forests grow in parts of Central and South America, Africa, India, and Southeast Asia, Australia, and New Guinea. Although rain forests in these different places have different kinds of plants and animals, a close look at these living things shows how much they have in common because they live in similar habitats.

Rain-forest Foods

Do you like bananas? What about tomatoes, chocolate, or pineapples? Many of the foods we eat used to grow only in rain forests. Now they are also grown on farms.

◄ Chocolate is made from the seeds of the cacao tree. The seeds are inside large tough-skinned fruits, called pods.

▼Ring-tailed lemurs

Layers of Life

A rain forest is divided into layers, from top to bottom. These layers are formed by its plants. Most plants in a rain forest are racing to reach the light from the sun. Plants compete with each other for light. That is because they use the energy in sunlight to make food. If a plant is in the shade of another plant, it is not getting all the light that it needs. Many rain-forest trees reach the sun by growing very tall. Their trunks lack branches for most of this height. At the top, the trees flare out into branches. The branches stretch up and sideways to expose their leaves to the sun. These tall trees are called **emergents**.

The emergents poke out of a layer of treetops called the **canopy**. The treetops' edges fit closely together like pieces in a jigsaw puzzle. This layer of greenery is so thick that a person in an airplane flying over it can't see into the forest below.

The canopy blocks sunlight from shining into the rain forest. It creates a shady zone called the **understory**. The understory is filled with small trees and some bushes. Some of the trees are full-grown. They are able to grow in the understory because they are shade lovers. Other trees are young trees of the same type as the canopy trees. They grow very slowly, waiting for a chance to shoot up toward the sunlight if a big tree falls down.

Vines and Lianas

Tying the layers together are ropelike plants called vines and **lianas** (lee-AH-nuhs). Vines have soft stems. Lianas have woody stems. Both kinds of plants loop in and out of branches and trunks as they try to reach the sunlight.

At the bottom is the forest floor. It is covered with mushrooms, other kinds of fungi, and smaller plants that like shade.

When a big tree falls, it often pulls down other trees because it is tied to them with vines and lianas. This opens up a hole in the canopy. Right away, understory plants start growing to fill up the space. Small trees that have waited for years to grow taller shoot toward the sky.

Some trees reach heights of up to 200 feet—as tall as a 20-story building.

Many trees and bushes in the understory have very wide, flat, floppy leaves. The leaves' size helps the plants catch as much sunlight as possible.

The maiden veil fungus appears at night, spreading its lacy veil.

Emergents

Canopy

Understory

Forest Floor

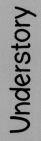

What It Means to Be Green in the Rain Forest

A rain forest presents many challenges to its plant life. A tree that pokes up above the others is blasted with hot sunshine and pounded by heavy rain. A plant that is lower down fights for its share of light. Over time, the plants have slowly changed in ways that help them live in this wet habitat. This kind of slow change is called **adaptation**.

One adaptation is the pointy tips that many rain-forest plants have on their leaves. They are called drip tips. Rain that falls on the leaf rolls across its smooth, waxy surface and is funneled to the drip tip. Then it rolls off the leaf. Having a drip tip helps keep a leaf from being covered with moss and other plants that might otherwise grow on it and block out light. Plants that grow on other plants are called **epiphytes** (EH-puh-fights). A rain-forest tree's trunk and branches are hung with epiphytes.

A field trip to the forest canopy is like visiting a garden! Ferns, mosses, and flowers called orchids grow in every nook and cranny. They perch on the trees, soaking up water and air from the atmosphere with their roots. They get **nutrients**—the food that they need in order to grow—from the pockets of dirt that settle around them over time. Vines and lianas spread through the trees, growing skyward in an effort to reach the light. Some climbing plants coil around trees. Others grow hooks that help them latch onto bark.

On the forest floor, plants are challenged, too. Rain-forest soil is very old. It is not rich in nutrients that plants need for growing. To get what they need, plants grow shallow roots that snake across the forest floor. These shallow roots soak up nourishment from the thin layer of dead leaves that covers the forest floor.

Even big trees have these shallow roots, so their roots do not help hold them up. Instead, the trees' trunks have giant bases, called **buttresses,** that spread out to support them.

Another challenge plants face are the other living things in the rain forest—the insects and other animals that eat them! But many plants also depend on animals to help make and spread their seeds.

The Strangler Fig

A plant called the strangler fig wraps around a tree's trunk as it grows. When it reaches the top, its leaves spread out and shade the tree. The tree dies because it can't get enough light, but the fig lives on.

The Giant Rafflesia

The giant rafflesia grows the world's largest flower. It is about 3 feet across. Its rotten-meat smell attracts the flies that help it grow seeds.

Leaf-cutter Ants

Leaf-cutter ants carry bits of leaves back to their nests. Later the ants will eat the fungus that grows on the stored leaves.

11

Incredible Insect Life

The rain forest is home to millions of species of insects. Scientists keep finding new rain-forest species, and they think there may be millions more kinds of insects still to be discovered.

Butterflies are among the most colorful insects. Many butterflies have wings that flash like jewels in the sunlight. Bright colors help butterflies of the same species find each other. Some brightly colored butterflies are also poisonous to eat. Their colors warn hungry animals to leave them alone.

Many butterflies feed on a sweet liquid called nectar that is made inside flowers. When a butterfly lands to feed, its body is dusted with a powder made by the flower. This powder is called pollen. The butterfly carries the pollen to the next flower it visits. The pollen sticks to a part of that flower that uses the pollen to make seeds. This process is called **pollination**.

Without insects, many rain-forest plants would not be pollinated. Other insects that pollinate plants are moths, flies, bees, wasps, and beetles.

▲ Blue morpho butterfly

▼ Anna's eighty-eight butterfly

▲ The Atlas moth is one of the world's largest moths. It is found in rain forests in parts of Southeast Asia.

Insect Disguises

Some rain-forest insects look like leaves or flowers. This "disguise" helps them blend in with plants so that predators can't find them. Insects called katydids that look like green leaves even have brown patches or "nibbled" edges—the kind of damage a real leaf often has.

▲ This katydid's spiny legs help protect it from being eaten if its green color fails to hide it.

Poisonous Plants

Many insects also eat leaves. Plants get rid of these leaf munchers. They may make poisons so that their leaves taste bad or even kill insects. Many insect species respond by becoming **immune** to the poison, which means it no longer harms them.

Some insects even use the plants' poisons to fight their own battles. Caterpillars of the passion-flower butterflies eat poisonous passion-flower plants. They store up the plants' poison in their own bodies. The poison is still there when they become butterflies. The butterflies' black, orange, and yellow wings let other animals know that they taste bad and contain poison. Other animals, like birds, quickly learn to avoid them.

◀Tiger longwing butterfly

Helpful Ants

Some plants team up with ants to keep caterpillars and other animals from eating their leaves. The plants provide special pockets of nectar just for ants. Some even grow little bundles of food for them on their leaves or provide hollow stems for ants to live in. The ants "pay back" the plant by swarming out to attack insects that try to eat it or lay eggs on it.

Creepy Crawlers

Living in the rain forest are other animals that, like insects, do not have skeletons inside their bodies. These animals are called **invertebrates**. Rain-forest invertebrates include centipedes, millipedes, spiders, and scorpions.

Insects and other invertebrates on the forest floor feed on dead leaves and the bodies of dead animals. By eating them, invertebrates help break them down into smaller bits that can be used by plants. Nutrients in the rain forest are constantly being recycled in this way.

A scorpion has a venomous sting in its tail for hunting and defense.

A Bird-eating Tarantula

One of the world's biggest spiders—the goliath bird-eating tarantula—lives in South American rain forests. This spider measures up to one foot across. Its fangs are one inch long, and its body is covered with bristles. At night, it hunts by sneaking up on **prey** that passes close to its burrow. The bird-eating tarantula rarely eats birds. It usually feeds on insects, frogs, lizards, and mice.

A goliath bird-eating ▶
tarantula uses its legs
to flick hairs off its body
and into the eyes and nose of
an animal that attacks it.

14

Enormous Millipedes

Millipedes feed on leaves and other plant parts that fall to the forest floor. One of the world's biggest millipedes, the giant African millipede, lives in rain forests in Africa. It can grow to be a foot long, with 200 to 300 legs.

Fewer Legs and Poisonous

Another large many-legged invertebrate is the giant centipede. It grows as long as the giant millipede, but doesn't have as many legs. It lives in South American rain forests, where it eats insects, worms, toads, snails, mice, and even bats. It uses its front pair of claws to grab prey and inject it with its venom, which is a strong poison.

▲ Millipedes roll up when they are threatened. They may also ooze a poisonous fluid.

The centipede's bright colors ▶ warn that it has a venomous bite.

Imitating Ants

Spiders in many rain forests look and act a lot like ants. They are called ant-mimicking spiders. These spiders have long, thin bodies that look like ants' bodies. Like all spiders, an ant mimic has eight legs, but it holds its extra-long two front legs up so that they look like an ant's antennae. Scientists think spiders imitate ants to defend themselves. Most birds do not like to eat ants because the tiny insects make a burning acid when they are attacked.

Fantastic Frogs

◀ Red-eyed tree frog

A frog can absorb water through its skin. It gets most of its water this way. It can also absorb oxygen through its skin. Even though a frog also breathes using its lungs, it needs this extra oxygen to survive. It needs to keep its skin moist so that it does not dry out. For a frog, the dim, damp world of the rain forest is the perfect habitat.

Some rain-forest frogs live in ponds and rivers, but many kinds live up in trees. Tree frogs have toes with suction pads at the tips. The pads also ooze a sticky fluid. With these sticky toes, a tree frog can easily cling to a tree trunk or even a leaf. Other frogs live among the leaves that litter the forest floor.

Frogs eat mainly insects, worms, and other small animals. Some species eat other frogs. Some large species also eat reptiles, small fish, and even mice. Frogs, in turn, are eaten by other animals.

Many frogs blend in with leaves. Others are brown and blend in with the forest floor. But many species are as eye-catching as butterflies, with colors such as tomato red and canary yellow!

Amazonian leaf frog ▶

The most brightly colored frogs are the poison dart frogs of Central and South America. Poison dart frogs are boldly patterned with splashes of blue, red, orange, yellow, or green striped with black. Their skin makes a poison so strong that just a tiny drop can kill a large animal. Their bright colors are a warning to other animals: "Don't eat me!"

Frogs fly through the air in some tropical rain forests in parts of Southeast Asia. These "flying" frogs are actually gliding. A flying frog's big feet have webbed toes. A flap of skin also runs along each side of its body. If a **predator** tries to catch it, the frog leaps out of a tree and spreads its toes and skin flaps wide. It glides on these "wings" to safety in another tree.

▼ Red poison dart frog

Poison Dart Frogs

A female poison dart frog carries her tadpoles on her back up a tree. She puts the babies into **bromeliads** (broe-MEE-lee-adds), epiphytes with leaves that form small cups. Rain collects in the cups. Lots of animals—including frogs—use these tiny pools in the treetops. Monkeys and birds drink from them. The female poison dart frog lets her babies swim in the plants' mini ponds. She returns every day to lay an egg in the water for each tadpole to eat. In Papua New Guinea, the males of two frog species guard the eggs and then carry the babies that hatch for up to nine days.

▲ Blue poison dart frog

Rain-Forest Reptiles

The flying dragon and the basilisk are not mythical creatures—they are just two of the fascinating reptiles that live in tropical rain forests.

The flying dragon lives in rain forests in parts of Southeast Asia. Its wings are red-and-brown-striped flaps of skin that stretch across rib bones on each side. Most of the time, its wings are folded up. When the lizard leaps into the air to glide to another tree, its wings open. Flying snakes also live in these rain forests.

The basilisk is a lizard that lives in the rain forests of Central America. It dives into the water below to escape predators. Then it stands up on its two hind legs and runs across the water's surface. It can run up to 15 feet—about half the length of a big school bus—in this way before it drops forward into the water and swims with all four legs.

◄ Basilisk

The Giant Anaconda

The world's biggest snake—the giant anaconda—lives in South American rain forests. It can grow to be 30 feet long—as long as a three-story building is high. Anacondas live near streams, rivers, ponds, and swamps. They hunt in the water. They lie in wait to catch small deer and other animals. An anaconda kills its prey by coiling around it. Each time the prey breathes out, the snake tightens its hold until the prey can no longer breathe in.

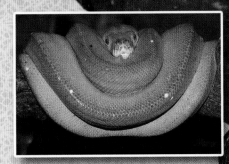

▲ Green tree python

Twin Snakes Living a World Apart

Many tree snakes in the rain forest are green. Two of these green snakes look like twins—but they live in different places and are not related. The green tree python lives in Papua New Guinea and parts of Southeast Asia. It is yellow or red as a baby and bright green as an adult. It sits on a branch with its body looped, coil over coil, like rope, resting its head in the middle. Half a world away in South America, the emerald tree boa drapes its green body over a branch in just the same way. Its babies are orange, brown, or yellow with spots.

▲ Emerald tree boa

◄ A chameleon can move each eye independently of the other.

Chameleons

About eighty species of chameleons are found in Africa. A few species are also found in southern Asia and around the Mediterranean. These lizards are famous for their ability to change color. But they don't change color in order to hide. Changing color is a way to "talk" to other chameleons. A threatened chameleon may go from leaf-green to a brighter color. This tells other chameleons to stay away.

19

River Life

Rain running down the trunks of rain-forest trees slowly finds its way into streams and rivers. These waterways provide habitats for many rain-forest animals, such as frogs and reptiles—and even a giant rodent and a mini hippopotamus! A variety of fish also live in the streams and rivers.

About 5,000 species of fish live in one of the world's mightiest rivers, the Amazon River of South America. The Amazon is about 4,000 miles long—longer than a trip from Chicago to London. One out of every five gallons of water flowing off the earth's land surface into the ocean is carried by the Amazon River. The huge Amazonian rain forest surrounds it.

Eels that Shock

In the Amazonian rain forest's dark, muddy waterways lives a fish that kills prey with electricity—the electric eel. This slim fish can grow to be nine feet long—three arms' lengths laid end to end. An electric eel produces electricity in organs inside its body, along its sides. These organs produce a jolt strong enough to knock out a human. This shocking ability is used to stun and kill fish, which are then sucked into the eel's mouth.

▲ Discus fish

The Black Caiman

Fish are eaten by a variety of rain-forest animals like the black caiman, a large South American reptile that lives along the Amazon River. This crocodile relative can grow up to 13 feet long. Besides fish, it also eats birds, turtles, and even deer. It is the largest predator in its habitat. In the past, it was hunted to near-extinction by people who wanted it for its meat and skin.

An eel may also give off electricity to defend itself against a predator. And it can use weak electrical bursts to find its way around in dim water.

Fish that Eat Cows

Another famous rain-forest fish is the piranha. There are about 25 different species of piranhas. A meat-eating piranha has a strong lower jaw that sticks out farther than its upper one. Each jaw is lined with razor-sharp teeth. Piranhas eat almost anything they meet in the water, such as fish, insects, and frogs. A big school of piranhas can even gobble up an unlucky cow that wanders into the water!

Plant-eating piranhas have longer jaws and blunter teeth. These fish eat leaves and other plant parts. They also sniff out fruit that has fallen from trees into the water. When the river overflows its banks during very rainy seasons and floods the rain forest, they join other fish in swimming toward the flooded land to feed on fruit. When they swim back, they carry the trees' seeds with them. Later, when waste matter passes out of the piranhas, the seeds will be dropped in places where they can grow.

Brilliant Birds

◀ Scarlet macaw

Scarlet macaw, rainbow lorikeet, golden parakeet—these are just a few of the birds that bring razzle-dazzle color to the world's rain forests, where thousands of species of birds live. Many are found nowhere else. Some rain-forest birds spend the summer north or south of the tropical zone and then fly to rain forests for the winter.

Parrots are the most famous rain-forest birds. There are more than 100 species of parrots. One of the biggest parrots is the scarlet macaw. It is about three feet long. Much of this length comes from its long tail feathers. Macaws have strong hooked beaks that can crack open hard nuts. They nest in tree holes.

Toucans share the macaws' Central and South American rain forests. Toucans have colorful beaks that can be as long as their bodies— sometimes even longer.

◀ Rainbow-billed toucan

The big beaks are lightweight and help toucans reach for fruit. Scientists think the bills also help toucans recognize others of the same species.

▲ Birds of paradise

In Papua New Guinea's rain forests, you can see birds of paradise. Male birds of paradise boast vivid colors and long fluffy or wiry plumes, which they show off when they try to attract a mate. The blue bird of paradise even flips upside down on a branch while displaying his feathers.

Rain-forest birds find plenty of insects and fruits to eat in their habitat. Many plants depend on birds to spread their seeds by eating their fruit, then leaving the seeds somewhere else in their droppings. Some plants rely on hummingbirds to carry pollen from flower to flower.

Rainbow ▶ lorikeet

◄ Toco toucan

▲ Ruby-throated hummingbird

Birds in Danger

Many species of rain-forest birds are in danger of becoming **extinct**. The main cause is habitat destruction. Birds lose their homes when rain forests are cut or burned down. Another problem is the capture of parrots for pets. In the past, more than one million birds a year were caught and sold as pets. Now many countries, such as the United States, have laws that make it illegal to take birds caught in the wild into the country to sell. But too many birds are still being caught illegally. Wildlife organizations and governments are working to stop this trade.

Blue-and- ▶ yellow macaw

Magnificent Mammals

Many different species of **mammals** can be found in the rain forest—and they live in all the layers.

High up in the understory and the canopy is the world of flying and climbing mammals. Fruit bats sniff out ripe fruits in the rain forests of Africa, Australia, and Southeast Asia.

Anteaters called tamanduas use their tails to help them climb among branches in the Amazonian rain forest. Sometimes they meet sloths—shaggy, slow-moving animals that spend their lives hanging upside down by their hooklike claws.

Many mammals creep, scurry, or trot across the forest floor. The biggest mammal of the forest floor in South America is the tapir. A tapir looks like a cross between a pig and a small hippo. It weighs up to 500 pounds—almost half as much as a milk cow. A tapir snuffles across the floor looking for plants to eat. It also swims and will dive into the water to escape from predators.

Smaller piglike animals called peccaries also feed on the forest floor. Another, even smaller plant eater, the agouti, comes out at night to eat. This cat-size rodent eats leaves and fruit. Like a squirrel, it buries nuts far and wide to eat later. Some of the seeds, however, are not found and grow into new trees.

▲ A ring-tailed lemur climbs trees but spends more time on the ground than other kinds of lemurs.

▲ Fruit bat

▲ A sloth's hooked claws are used as hangers and also as defensive weapons.

▼ Peccary

◄ A baby tapir has stripes. It loses them as it grows up.

▲ Tigers like to splash and paddle in water even when they are not hunting.

▲ The jaguar's spots help **camouflage** it.

Agoutis, peccaries, and tapirs are preyed on by big spotted cats called jaguars. Jaguars often hunt near rivers. In the past, jaguars were hunted for their fur. They disappeared from some places. Today, jaguars are mainly threatened by the loss of their habitat. They are also sometimes shot by cattle ranchers. Jaguars are now protected by law in many countries.

Big striped cats prowl Southeast Asian rain forests—tigers! Tigers prey on black-and-white tapirs and many species of deer. A very small deer that looks like an agouti shares its habitat. This deer, called the mouse deer, dives into water just like a tapir if it is frightened.

◀ Agouti

The Capybara

The world's biggest rodent, the capybara, lives in the Amazonian rain forest. It is about the size of a big German shepherd dog. A capybara lives around water and feeds on plants. Its feet are partly webbed to help it swim.

25

▲ Spider monkey

Monkey Business

Monkeys live in rain forests in Central and South America, Africa, and parts of Asia. Most monkeys of the Americas can do something that African and Asian monkeys can't. They can hang by their tails and use them as extra hands or feet. A tail like this is called a **prehensile tail**.

The spider monkey's tail is especially long—about one and a half times as long as the monkey's body! In fact, it is called a spider monkey because, with its thin arms and legs, it looks like a spider when it hangs by its tail. Spider monkeys spend their lives in the canopy and rarely visit the forest floor.

Sharing the canopy with them are other species of monkeys. Howler monkeys are named for their loud voices. A howler monkey's call can be heard nearly two miles away. Tiny squirrel monkeys skitter among the branches, searching for figs and insects. At night, monkeys called douroucoulis (DEWR-uh-KOO-lees) come out to feed. They are the only monkeys in the world that are active at night and asleep during the day.

In some South American rain forests, little monkeys called marmosets and tamarins search for insects, fruit, and tree sap in the canopy.

◄ Squirrel monkey

▲ Howler monkey

Species include the emperor tamarin, which has a splendid white mustache, and the common marmoset, which has puffs of white hair on the sides of its head.

Africa's rain-forest monkeys include the world's largest monkey, the mandrill. A male mandrill has a bright blue-and-red face. Mandrills spend most of their time on the forest floor. Asia's rain-forest monkeys include the proboscis (pruh-BAH-suss) monkey. Males of this species have giant floppy noses that make their honking calls extra loud. Proboscis monkeys often dive from high branches onto lower ones. They also drop down into swamps and rivers, landing with a crash on their bellies.

◀ A mandrill stores food in its cheek pouches so it can carry its meal to a safe spot, where it takes its time chewing.

The Golden Lion Tamarin

The golden lion tamarin has a yellow-orange coat and a fluffy mane. This monkey lives in Brazil. Only about 1,500 now live in the wild. They are endangered because most of their forest has been cut down. Some areas are now protected as reserves for tamarins and other animals.

The Pygmy Marmoset

The world's smallest monkey, the pygmy marmoset, lives in rain forests in parts of South America. It is only a foot long, with its tail making up half that length.

27

◄ Gorilla

Amazing Apes

The ape family includes gorillas, chimpanzees, bonobos, orangutans, and gibbons. Apes are found in the rain forests of Asia and Africa. They do not live in South America, Australia, or New Guinea.

Gorillas are the biggest apes. They live on the forest floor of rain forests in central Africa, where they feed on leaves. Gorillas travel in groups made up of a few females, their babies, and a male who is the leader. He is the boss of any other males in the group, too.

Some gorillas sleep in trees but otherwise rarely climb them. The other African apes—chimpanzees and their cousins, bonobos—divide their time between the ground and trees of the understory.

Apes in Trouble

All apes are endangered species because of the cutting of rain forests. Governments in some countries are working to set aside reserves for apes. Zoos are trying to raise some apes in captivity to save the species.

▲ Bonobo mother and baby

Chimpanzees eat fruit as well as leaves and insects. They sometimes kill and eat monkeys and antelopes, too. Chimps are also toolmakers. A chimp that wants to catch termites picks up a twig and nibbles off its leaves. Then it pushes the twig into holes in a termite mound. After angry termites crawl onto the twig, the chimp pulls it out and slurps up the insects.

Asia's rain-forest apes—gibbons and orangutans—use their arms to swing from branch to branch in the canopy. An orangutan is almost as big as a gorilla. A gibbon is about as tall as a two-year-old child. But its arms are almost twice as long as its body.

Male orangutans live on their own, searching for fruit to eat. Female orangutans travel with their babies, who cling to their mothers' fur with their hands. Gibbons form pairs that stay together.

▼ Orangutan

The Gibbon

Some gibbon species can zip through the trees at speeds of up to 35 miles per hour. A gibbon sometimes lets go at the end of a swing and sails through the air to land on a branch 30 feet away. Pairs of gibbons often call back and forth to each other for many minutes at a time. This behavior is called singing or duetting. The female usually starts the singing, and the male responds. Their calls can be heard half a mile away.

New Rain-Forest Animals

Many experts say that rain forests have not yet revealed all their secrets. It is thought that there are many more animals still to be discovered in the world's rain forests. Some of these animals may be known only to the native peoples of the rain forests, while others may have never been seen by human eyes.

Scientists believe that about 50 percent of the world's plant and animal species live in rain forests, which take up only 7 percent of the earth's surface. They think that many more rain-forest plants and animals are still undiscovered—especially in Papua New Guinea and central Africa.

Many of the new species that scholars find in rain forests are insects. Some newly discovered insects are still waiting to be named! But larger animals are also turning up.

The Okapi

The okapi is a mammal about the size of a horse. It is related to the giraffe and lives in the rain forest of Zaire, an African country. African people in the area knew about it, but European explorers did not see one until 1900. The okapi's name comes from an African word for this animal. An okapi has a long, dark gray tongue that it uses to rip leaves from branches. The tongue is so long that an okapi can clean its own ears with it! The male okapi has skin-covered horns on its head. The female is slightly taller than the male.

In 2005, scientists exploring in a New Guinea rain forest discovered many new species, including frogs, butterflies, and birds.

In 2006, about 40 new species of plants and animals were discovered in the Amazonian rain forest. Among them were a tree rat the size of a guinea pig and a bird. These discoveries show just how little is really known about rain forests and how much more there is to learn.

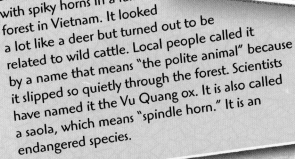

The Vu Quang Ox

In 1992, explorers found another new large mammal with spiky horns in a rain forest in Vietnam. It looked a lot like a deer but turned out to be related to wild cattle. Local people called it by a name that means "the polite animal" because it slipped so quietly through the forest. Scientists have named it the Vu Quang ox. It is also called a saola, which means "spindle horn." It is an endangered species.

Miniature Night Frog

Scientists exploring a rain forest in India found a new species of frog hidden among fallen leaves. The frog belongs to a group of species called night frogs. They gave it a scientific name that means "the smallest night frog." Males of this species are less than half an inch long. They are small enough to sit comfortably on a coin about the size of a nickel.

▲ A field researcher. Scientists and other interested people go to field stations around the world to study rain forests.

The Black-headed Sagui Dwarf

In 1996, a scientist discovered a new kind of monkey in Brazil. It was given to him by a local person who did not know it was an unknown species. The little monkey is now called the black-headed sagui dwarf. It is about four inches long. It is the second-smallest monkey in the world. The smallest is the pygmy marmoset. The sagui dwarf lives in an area of the Amazonian rain forest about the size of Rhode Island.

31

People and Rain Forests

▲ Hut along the eroding banks of the Rio Napo in the rain forest in Ecuador.

Today there are still people in the rain forests who live as their ancestors did. Other people live around rain forests. All together, about half a billion people still live in or near rain forests and use them for food, firewood, and other basic needs.

But as the human population has grown, the amount of rain forest in the world has shrunk. This is partly because people living around the edges have chopped away at it to plant crops.

Long ago, people living at the edge of the forest would cut down trees and burn them to clear patches of land for farming. When the land was no longer able to produce good crops, the farmers moved on to clear another patch. When a rain forest is cut down so the land can be used for crops, the soil is good only for a year or two. Then it is of little use for farming anymore. This did not harm the forests, because there was lots of forest and not that many people. Today the forests do suffer harm because there are many more people trying to live that way.

Large businesses have also destroyed rain forests. Rain forests have been cut down to make logs and paper.

In Central and South America, rain forests have been cut down to make pastures for beef cattle. Mining for minerals such as gold has also destroyed forests.

The Annatto Tree

People have lived in rain forests for thousands of years. They know how to use the plants that grow there. The annatto tree grows in the Amazonian rain forest. Native people make face paint from it, which they use as a natural sunblock and snake repellent.

Rain Forests and the Earth

Some scientists say the rain forests may be gone in fifty years. But many people are working hard to make sure that this does not happen.

Some countries are making stronger rules about logging the forests. They are also setting aside forests to protect them. Some countries are also working to help poor people farm without destroying the forests.

People are becoming more aware that destroying rain forests does more than just make beautiful places disappear. Rain forests are part of the different cycles that shape the earth's weather and its water supply.

Rain forests affect weather because they give off water and cool the air. A rain forest makes about half the rain that falls on it. This happens because plants and soil give off water that slowly seeps into the air. This water later forms clouds and falls again as rain.

Rain-forest Medicines

Some rain-forest plants have been used to create medicines. Scientists think that many more chemicals that could cure diseases may lie hidden in rain-forest plants.

The wetness and shade of a rain forest also help cool the air. Without rain forests, sunlight can warm the ground and air and make it hotter. Land cleared of rain forest also reflects more sunlight than a dark forest canopy does. This causes the air to heat up, too.

Rain forests also stop hard rains from pounding the soil and washing it away. This is important because rain forests have so little rich soil in the first place. The amount of rain forest that is destroyed every year adds up to an area about the size of North Carolina. Burning rain forests pour lots of a gas called carbon dioxide into the air. This gas traps heat. If carbon dioxide levels rise too high, the earth's atmosphere may get too warm and dry in the future.

Rain forests cover just a small portion of the earth, but half of all plant and animal species live in them. People who live in and near rain forests, as well as people who live far away, are just starting to learn how to take care of this habitat so that it will be there to use and enjoy in the future.

Glossary

adaptation: the way a plant or animal changes over a very long period of time to survive better in its environment

bromeliad: a plant that grows on other plants and has cuplike leaves that catch rainwater

buttress: a tree trunk that has grown much wider at the bottom, which helps support the tree

camouflage: the way an animal or plant blends in with its background so a predator cannot see it

canopy: the tops of tall trees in a rain forest

emergent: a very tall tree that pokes above the rain-forest canopy

epiphyte: a plant that grows on another plant

equator: an imaginary line around the middle of the earth halfway between the North and South Poles

extinct: when a species of plant or animal no longer exists

habitat: where a plant or animal naturally lives; the best place for it to survive

immune: protected against a poison or disease

invertebrate: an animal that does not have a skeleton inside its body

liana: a woody vine that wraps around other plants

mammal: a warm-blooded animal that drinks milk from its mother when it is born

nutrient: an element in an animal or plant's food that nourishes it

pollination: the way insects carry pollen from one flower to another, which causes the second flower to make seeds

predator: an animal that eats other animals

prehensile tail: a tail that can be used like an arm or leg

prey: an animal that is eaten by other animals

species: a group of animals or plants that have enough things in common to be able to reproduce

tropics: areas of the world just north and south of the equator

understory: the layer of small trees and bushes below the canopy, or top, of the rain forest

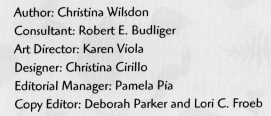

Author: Christina Wilsdon
Consultant: Robert E. Budliger
Art Director: Karen Viola
Designer: Christina Cirillo
Editorial Manager: Pamela Pia
Copy Editor: Deborah Parker and Lori C. Froeb

Images from Shutterstock.com:

Front cover: scarlet macaw, Kisa F. Young; blue morpho butterfly, Holger Wulschlaeger; yellow-banded poison-dart frog, Eric Isselée; red-eyed tree frog, Sascha Burkard; toco toucan, Lori Froeb; millipede, "Socrates"; bromeliad, Kato Inowe; baby jaguar, Ronnie Howard.
Pp. 4–5: tree, Joe Gough; fruit bat, Javarman; rainbow lorikeet, M. Willis; blue morpho butterfly, Ishmael Montero Verdu; Amazonian leaf frog, Dr. Morley Read. Pp. 6–7: background view of mountains and forest, Joe Gough; red flower, Ilya D. Gridnew; hummingbird, iDesign; bananas, Barbara Ayrapetyan; pineapple, Bogac Erguvenc; cacao pods, Dr. Morley Read; chocolate, Danny Smythe; ring-tailed lemurs, ivvv1975; blue-and-yellow macaw, Gila R. Todd; blue morpho butterfly, Ishmael Montero Verdu. Pp. 8–9: blue-and-yellow macaw, Sergei Chumakov; maiden veil fungus, large leaf, Amazonian tree, and liana, Dr. Morley Read; emergent trees (left), Dr. Morley Read; emergent trees (right), Joe Gough; background, Dimitry Savinov; baby jaguar, Ronnie Howard. Pp. 10–11: Amazonian tree with buttress roots, Dr. Morley Read; strangler fig, Craig Hill; giant rafflesia, Vova Pomortzeff; bird of paradise flower, Moremi. Pp. 12–13: blue morpho butterfly, Ishmael Montero Verdu; butterflies, Ishmael Montero Verdu; katydid, ants on branch, and leaf-mimic katydids, Dr. Morley Read; Atlas moth, Maggie. Pp. 14–15: scorpion, Dr. Morley Read; millipede, "Socrates"; centipede and Goliath bird-eating tarantula, John Bell. Pp. 16–17: red-eyed tree frog, Sascha Burkhard; yellow-banded poison-dart frog, Eric Isselée; red poison-dart frog, Steffen Foerster Photography; bromeliad, Kato Inowe; blue poison-dart frog, John Arnold; Amazonian leaf frog, Dr. Morley Read. Pp. 18–19: basilisk, Michael Zysman; green tree python, Timothy Craig Lubcke; chameleon (right), infografick; chameleon (left), Sebastian Duda; giant anaconda, Zvonimir Orec. Pp. 20–21: discus fish, Ljupco Smokovski; eels, Andy Heyward; piranha, Peter Jochems; black caiman, Dr. Morley Read. Pp. 22–23: scarlet macaw, Lisa F. Young; blue-and-yellow macaws in flight, Sergei Chumakov; rainbow lorikeet, M. Willis; caged blue-and-yellow macaw, Gila R. Todd; toco toucan, Lori Froeb; ruby-throated hummingbird, Ronnie Howard; rainbow-billed toucan, Michael Strzelecki. Pp. 24–25: ring-tailed lemur, Petr Maseki; fruit bat, Javarman; tiger, Cristina Ferrari; jaguar, Ronnie Howard; capybara, Pontus Edenberg; agouti and peccary, Vasiliy Koval; baby tapir, Holger Ehlers; sloth, Grigory Kubatyan. Pp. 26–27: golden lion tamarin, Howard Sandler; pygmy marmoset, Michael Lynch; mandrill, Van Hart; howler monkey, Jaana Piira; squirrel monkey, Louis Louro. Pp. 28–29: gorilla, Eric Gevaert; chimpanzee, Kitch Bain; gibbons, Timothy Craig Lubcke; orangutan, Shootov Igor; bonobos, Ronald van der Beek. Pp. 30–31: okapi, Judy Worley; field researcher, Vera Bogaerts. Pp. 32–33: huts along Rio Napo, Dr. Morley Read; woman with painted face, rsfatt; rain forest burning hut, Daniel Wiedemann; logs, Jose AS Reyes. P. 34: medicine bottle and cloves, Margaret M. Stewart; mortar and pestle, Andi Berger.
Diorama imagery: artis777, CarpathianPrince, enciktat, Dirk Ercken, leungchopan, Xico Putini, Ivan Smuk, Matt Tilghman.
Stickers: John Bell, Holger Ehlers, Lori Froeb, R. Gino Santa Maria, Ronnie Howard, iDesign, Eric Isselée, ivvv1975, Javarman, lightpoet, Maggie, Jaana Piira, Dr. Morley Read, "Socrates", Michael Strzelecki, Gila R. Todd, Ishmael Montero Verdu, M.Willis, Judy Worley, Holger Wulschlaeger.

Images from istockphoto.com:

P. 13: tiger longwing butterfly, Karl Blessing; P. 15: ant-mimicking spider, James Benet. P. 26: spider monkey, ODM Studio. P. 27: emperor tamarin, Kevdog818. Pp. 34–35: aerial view of Amazon rain forest, Brasil2.

Illustrations by Jill Bauman:

© Reader's Digest Children's Publishing, Inc.
P. 31: Vu Quang ox, miniature night frog, black-headed sagui dwarf.

3-D model art by Steve Roberts/Wildlife Art (praying mantis, monarch butterly, monarch caterpillar)

3-D Model Instructions

Complete one puzzle at a time. Press out the pieces and arrange them as shown. Using the numbers on the pictures here, match the slots and assemble your 3-D rain forest animals.

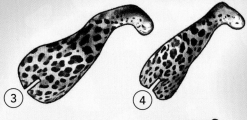

Jaguar

The jaguar's spots help camouflage it.

Praying Mantis

Female mantises sometimes eat the male mantises during mating.

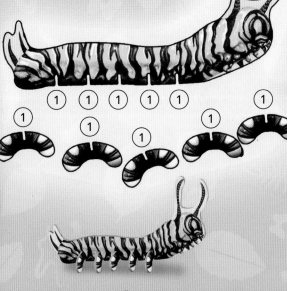

Monarch Caterpillar

These caterillars eat only milkweed—
making them poisonous to predators.

Monarch Butterfly

Some monarch butterflies migrate over
2,000 miles to find a warmer climate.

Blue-and-Yellow Macaw

The blue-and-yellow macaw has only one
mate, with whom it stays for life.

Diorama Instructions

Bring your own rain forest to life by building a beautiful diorama. It's easy!

box lid

box base

1. The inside of the box lid and base will be the walls of your diorama. The unfolding board will be the floor. Decorate these with reusable stickers as desired.

stickers

unfolding board

2. Press out the floor figures, and fold as shown. The tips of the ferns can be curled for a nice effect. Fold, then slide the rectangular tabs through the floor slots, folding them underneath so the figures stand upright. The tabs and slots are all the same size, so you can change the position of the figures.

floor figures

3. Stand the box lid and base upright and at an angle as shown. Lay the angled back e es of the floor piece on top of the box sides. You're done!